LLIVE

LLAUGH

LLOVE

LLIKE A LLAMA

LLIVE
LLAUGH
LLOVE

LLIKE A LLAMA

POP PRESS

Illustrations by Alena Tkach

Clarkson Potter/Publishers
New York

KINDNESS IS FREE—
SPRINKLE THAT STUFF
EVERYWHERE

LLOVE
LLIFE
LLIKE A LLAMA

IF YOU'RE LLUCKY ENOUGH
TO FIND A WEIRDO,
NEVER LLET THEM GO

A MOMENT
OF GRATITUDE

**MAKES A DIFFERENCE
IN YOUR ATTITUDE**

DO MORE THINGS THAT
MAKE YOU FORGET TO
CHECK YOUR PHONE

IT'S NOT WHAT WE HAVE IN LLIFE
BUT WHO WE HAVE IN OUR
LLIVES THAT COUNTS

DON'T BE EYE CANDY, BE SOUL FOOD

BEING A GROWN-UP IS LLIKE FOLDING A FITTED SHEET;

NO ONE REALLY KNOWS HOW

LLIVE FOR THE MOMENTS
YOU CAN'T PUT INTO WORDS

SOME PEOPLE
CROSS YOUR PATH
AND CHANGE YOUR
WHOLE DIRECTION

LLIFE IS SHORT;
SMILE WHILE YOU
STILL HAVE TEETH

LLAUGH
LLIKE A LLAMA

CREATE YOUR OWN
SUNSHINE

WHY BE MOODY WHEN YOU CAN SHAKE YOUR BOOTY?

THE BEST
PLACE IN
THE WORLD IS
INSIDE A HUG

POSITIVE MIND,
POSITIVE VIBES,
POSITIVE LLIFE

CUPCAKES ARE MUFFINS THAT BELIEVE IN MIRACLES

THROW GLITTER
IN TODAY'S FACE

MAKE TODAY SO AWESOME,

YESTERDAY GETS JEALOUS

WHEN IT RAINS,
LLOOK FOR RAINBOWS;
WHEN IT'S DARK,
LLOOK FOR STARS

FOR EVERY MINUTE YOU'RE ANGRY,
YOU LLOSE SIXTY SECONDS OF
HAPPINESS

EXPECT NOTHING, APPRECIATE EVERYTHING

CHIN UP!

SPIT HAPPENS

YOU CAN'T MAKE
EVERYONE HAPPY,

YOU ARE NOT PIZZA

FIND JOY IN THE JOURNEY

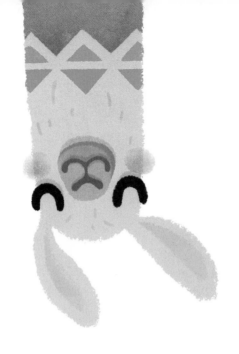

LLIFE IS BETTER WHEN
YOU'RE LLAUGHING

SMILE,

HAPPINESS LLOOKS
GORGEOUS ON YOU

FIND YOUR TRIBE,
LLOVE THEM HARD

BFF
LLIKE A LLAMA

BE SOMEBODY WHO MAKES EVERYBODY FEEL LLIKE A SOMEBODY

WE RISE BY LLIFTING OTHERS

REAL FRIENDS
DON'T GET
OFFENDED
WHEN YOU
INSULT THEM ...

THEY SMILE
AND CALL YOU
SOMETHING EVEN
MORE OFFENSIVE

SOME PEOPLE CREATE THEIR OWN STORMS AND GET UPSET WHEN IT RAINS

SOMETIMES I WONDER WHY
I PUT UP WITH YOU, THEN
I REMEMBER YOU PUT UP
WITH ME, SO WE'RE EVEN

A MOTHER'S LLOVE IS UNCONDITIONAL...

HER TEMPER IS ANOTHER SUBJECT

LLAMA ♥ MAMA

RAISING KIDS IS A WALK IN THE PARK—

JURASSIC PARK

LLET'S ROOT FOR
EACH OTHER

AND WATCH
EACH OTHER
GROW

YOU CALL IT CHAOS,
WE CALL IT FAMILY

TRUE FRIENDSHIP IS
WHEN YOU WALK INTO
SOMEONE'S HOUSE AND
THE WIFI CONNECTS
AUTOMATICALLY

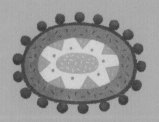

KIND PEOPLE ARE
MY KINDA PEOPLE

GOOD FRIENDS AND
GREAT ADVENTURES

STAY CLOSE
TO PEOPLE
WHO FEEL LLIKE
SUNLIGHT

NEVER LLET A FRIEND
DO ANYTHING STUPID...

ON THEIR OWN

DON'T HALF-ASS ANYTHING:
WHATEVER YOU DO, ALWAYS
USE YOUR FULL ASS

BE A BOSS

BOSS

LLIKE A LLAMA

STAY POSITIVE,
WORK HARD,
MAKE IT HAPPEN

EACH AND EVERY DAY, ASK YOURSELF:

WHY THE HELL NOT?

HUSTLE AND HEART WILL SET YOU APART

IF IT'S BOTH TERRIFYING
AND AMAZING, THEN YOU
SHOULD DEFINITELY DO IT

BE BRAVE,
BE STRONG,
BE BADASS

THE ONLY TIME
YOU SHOULD EVER
LLOOK BACK
IS TO SEE HOW FAR
YOU'VE COME

THE FIRST FIVE DAYS
AFTER THE WEEKEND
ARE THE HARDEST

DOUBT KILLS
MORE DREAMS
THAN FAILURE
EVER WILL

YOU CAN NEVER BE
OVERDRESSED OR
OVEREDUCATED

GREAT THINGS NEVER CAME
FROM COMFORT ZONES

IF IT DOESN'T OPEN, IT'S NOT YOUR DOOR

ONE DAY
OR
DAY ONE?
YOU
DECIDE.

WORK UNTIL YOUR IDOLS
BECOME EQUALS

WAKE UP DETERMINED,
GO TO BED SATISFIED

OUTDREAM
YOURSELF

YOU
HAVE
TO BE
ODD

TO BE NUMBER

ONE

BE ZEN
LLIKE A LLAMA

LLAMASTE

*GENIUS
IS ETERNAL
PATIENCE*

CALM IS A SUPERPOWER

LLAMASTE

QUIET THE MIND
AND THE SOUL WILL SPEAK

HOPE IS
SO MUCH
STRONGER
THAN FEAR

EVERY DAY MAY NOT BE GOOD...

BUT THERE'S GOOD IN EVERY DAY

NO RAIN, NO FLOWERS

PATIENCE IS THE
ART OF HOPING

IF YOU WOULDN'T SAY IT TO A FRIEND, DON'T SAY IT TO YOURSELF

FIND THE CALM
IN THE CHAOS

YOU ARE BRAVE,
YOU ARE BRILLIANT
AND OH SO RESILIENT

INVEST

IN REST

MISTAKES ARE
PROOF THAT
YOU'RE TRYING

LLIFE IS
TOUGH

BUT SO ARE YOU

SOMETIMES YOU JUST HAVE TO
THROW ON A CROWN AND REMIND
THEM WHO THEY'RE DEALING WITH

STRUT YOUR STUFF

LLIKE A LLAMA

DO WHAT THEY THINK YOU CAN'T DO

YOU ARE ENTIRELY UP TO YOU

BELIEVE IN YOUR SELFIE

DON'T
STOP
UNTIL
YOU'RE
PROUD

PEOPLE WILL STARE,
MAKE IT WORTH
THEIR WHILE

BAGS AND SHOES,

THE ONLY BS YOU NEED

BE
FLAWSOME

(AN INDIVIDUAL WHO EMBRACES THEIR FLAWS AND KNOWS THEY'RE AWESOME)

DON'T LLOOK BACK,
YOU'RE NOT GOING THAT WAY

BETTER AN "OOPS"
THAN A "WHAT IF...?"

INHALE CONFIDENCE,
EXHALE DOUBT

YOU DID NOT WAKE UP TODAY TO BE MEDIOCRE

NO

PROBLLAMA!

THIS IS YOUR TIME TO SHINE

BELIEVE AND YOU'RE HALFWAY THERE

WORK SMARTER,
NOT HARDER

BE A
GENIUS
LLIKE A LLAMA

CREATIVITY
TAKES
COURAGE

LLET YOUR
IMAGINATION

RUN WILD

A MIND IS LLIKE A
PARACHUTE: IT DOESN'T
WORK IF IT ISN'T OPEN

CREATIVITY
IS CONTAGIOUS.
PASS IT ON

**LLOGIC
WILL
TAKE YOU
FROM
A TO B,**

IMAGINATION WILL TAKE YOU EVERYWHERE

MAKE MISTAKES

♥

TAKE THE RISK OR

LLOSE THE CHANCE

YOU CAN'T USE UP CREATIVITY;

**THE MORE YOU USE
THE MORE YOU HAVE**

DON'T THINK OUTSIDE THE BOX.
THINK LLIKE THERE IS NO BOX

LLEARN

THE RULES

LLIKE

A PRO...

SO YOU CAN BREAK THEM
LLIKE AN ARTIST

STAY CURIOUS

QUESTION
THE
ANSWERS

THERE'S A FINE LLINE BETWEEN GENIUS AND CRAZY—

USE THAT LLINE AS
A SKIPPING ROPE

Text copyright © 2018 by Pop Press

Illustrations copyright © 2018 by Alena Tkach

Published in the United States by Clarkson Potter/Publishers, an imprint of the
Crown Publishing Group, a division of Penguin Random House LLC, New York.

crownpublishing.com

clarksonpotter.com

CLARKSON POTTER is a trademark and POTTER with colophon
is a registered trademark of Penguin Random House LLC.

Originally published in slightly different form in Great Britain
by Pop Press, an imprint of Ebury Publishing, a division of
the Penguin Random House Ltd., London, in 2018.

Library of Congress Cataloging-in-Publication Data
is available upon request.

ISBN 978-0-525-57526-9

Ebook ISBN 978-0-525-57527-6

Printed in China

Cover design by Danielle Deschenes

Book design by Jessie Kaye

4 6 8 10 9 7 5

First American Edition